PATINA

PATINA

A CHANGE PRODUCED BY LONG-STANDING BEHAVIOR, PRACTICE, OR USE

STEPHANIE CHERRY

Pleasant Word

Pleasant Word (a division of WinePress Publishing, PO Box 428, Enumclaw, WA 98022) functions only as book publisher. As such, the ultimate design, content, editorial accuracy, and views expressed or implied in this work are those of the author.

Unless otherwise noted, all Scripture references are taken from the Holy Bible, New American Standard Bible, © 1960, 1963, 1968, 1971, 1972, 1973, 1975, 1977 by The Lockman Foundation. Used by permission.

Scripture references marked KJV are taken from the King James Version of the Bible.

ISBN 1-4141-0826-5
Library of Congress Catalog Card Number: 2006907475

This work came to me mostly as God has woken me up to speak to me at 3 and 4 A.M. It is largely unedited because I wanted to share it, not to show off writing style, but share with you exactly what the Holy Spirit spoke to me in the wording He used to speak to me. This is a simple word given to help people who want to hear God's Word on a base level. It is written for the common traveler, for those looking for a change in all aspects. I have asked that each reader become a manifestation of the glory of Christ in their every day life. My only thanksgiving is to Jesus Christ and all those He has lent me. My heart's cry is to please Him.

Day 1

Jude 1:24

"Now to Him who is able to keep you from stumbling, and make you stand in the presence of His glory blameless with great joy."

Ladies, draw near to the three great gifts in this passage: God, blamelessness, and joy. Jude knew how to get it all in one sentence didn't he! Let's take a close look at each one separately.

To Him who is able to keep you from stumbling: God can keep you from stumbling. Soak that in, Sister! He doesn't offer to be the lead weight on all the things you've stuffed down inside. He offers to radically change your heart and mind. Believe that He can. Believe. Leave it all, "To the only God, our Savior, through Jesus Christ our Lord, be glory, majesty, dominion and authority before all time now and forever." (verse 25) Leave all that is unwashed in your house at His feet today. He who has called you is capable, faithful, and pure to cleanse all things you relinquish to Him.

He offers you that purity today. Blamelessness. He will call you blameless. Can you imagine? You can be fully washed in the water of the Word. I pray you a heart of conviction that leads to cleansing confession and repentance. If I could claim for you all the intimate gifts the Savior desires to lavish on you right now, I would. There is a theme to the relationship though. It is throughout Old Testament scripture. There is something you must do. "Return to Me and I will return to you." It does not say return to me and be perfect. Not, return to me and do the best job possible given the circumstances. Just come home. Turn it all over to Him. Ask Him. He will say, "yes."

Lastly, one of my favorite fruits of the Spirit is joy! Who couldn't use some of that? Please ask Him to never stop filling you with it! I encourage you to exercise and apply it to everything possible. Do a silly dance in the kitchen. Sing along with Veggie Tales. Play in the dirt. God made them all for you...

PS Eat some cheesecake.

My prayer over you today: Jude 2 "May mercy and peace and love be multiplied to you."

Chick Tip of the Day:

Do: Paint your toenails.
Don't wear chipped polish or pantyhose with sandals.

DAY 2

John 13:35

"By this all men will know you are my disciples, if you have love for one another."

Love: Releasing others to the God who is.

Are you clinging to the idea of saving or fixing someone in your own power?

One thing that ministered to me was when I began to truly grasp the meaning of scripture that says "God is Love." It is easy to say, but take a moment to breathe that in. God, in the core of His nature is Love. Pray the Living Word opens this truth to you. It will change everything.

Something I like to do in tough situations is write out scripture pertaining to what I am dealing with in love. I then replace the word love with God. In the second part of the above scripture it would say, "if you have God for one another." The love of Christ is always easier to pour out than trying to force our own flesh driven simulation of love. The hard part is when we bring Christ into the situation, He is quick to point out where we also have been unlovable.

Convictions of our own critical thoughts aren't easy to chew, swallow, or process. I pray you accept His offer and leap into the refiner's fire. Remember that all God offers everyone else He also offers to you. God is love to you. Every pure, unselfish, unconditional twinge of emotion (no matter how small it may seem) is a truly active God working through you. It makes your relationships seem a tad bit more important. It causes your efforts to seem more special. You freely give Christ to people through your very own heart! You don't have to take everyone down the Roman Road (salvation plan) for them to see and know the nature of God is pure, undefiled love.

John 13:20 "Truly, truly I say to you, he who receives whomever I send receives Me, and he who receives Me receives Him who sent Me."

Who are you in need to show God to today?

Have you asked Christ to show you the difference in His love and yours?

If so, have you asked Him to completely empty you of worldly love and fill you with Himself? Take that opportunity.

"Love one another." John 13:34

Chick Tip of the Day

Do: Wax. It's a simple thing to do for a pick me up.
Don't: Wax your lip for the first time, on your own!

DAY 3

⸻⁂

Proverbs 11:28

> Whomever trusts in his riches will fall,
> but the righteous will thrive like a green leaf.

Malachi 3:10

> Bring all the tithes (the whole tenth of your income) into the storehouse, that there may be food in My house, and prove Me now by it, says the Lord of hosts, if I will not open the windows of heaven for you and pour you out a blessing, that there shall not be room enough to receive it.

I think I may step on some tender toes today, but I ask that you bear with me. Let me ask you this: Are you tithing? I mean more than money, sister. I mean possessions and time. How much are you giving to God? Are you offering the first 10 percent of your day to God? He will multiply the time in your day. What is getting in your way? Not enough time? I could tell you that you don't have enough time to not meet with Him, but I fear it would just conjure up a critical spirit. That is what it did for me. I, too, used to not have enough time—except occasionally at the end of "my" day. Why does that plague so many Christians?

One day something changed in me, and the Spirit began to open up a new thought to me as I shared with a friend who was suffering from peculiar morning grumpiness. I gave her a copy of a favorite song of mine by Nichole Nordeman called "Mercies New". I would always sing it (read this carefully) "Your mercies are new every morning. I will wake with the dawn."

When we share things with others, the Spirit makes what seems so clear, even more so. (Anyone know what I am talking about?) For the first time, I heard what she was really saying: "Let me wake with the dawn." Let me. This isn't a struggle at all. It is simply something that I cannot do in my own power. It is the direct result of a desire, through prayer, to seek the favor and blessing of an intimate relationship with Jesus.

My suggestion to you is crazy, but quit trying to get up. Leave your need to do it with Christ and sing sweetly with me, "Let me." See if He doesn't shift the working of things to meet you. See if the mountainous region of doubt and valley fear and inadequacy aren't completely destroyed by your groom whose jealousy to meet with you cannot be rivaled. He will let you wake with the dawn.

Ask God to make you aware of how His mercies are new to you today. I pray you the favor and blessing of God to find perfect balance in every day He gives you. May yours truly be a lifestyle of prayer.

Chick Tip of the Day

Do: Get a manicure (it's nice to see pretty hands journaling about what you study in your Bible)

Don't: Get that French manicure at home kit. It doesn't work for anyone.

DAY 4

⟜⫘◯

1 Peter 5:6-8

"Humble yourselves, therefore, under God's mighty hand, that he may lift you up in due time. Cast all your anxiety on him because he cares for you. Be self-controlled and alert. Your enemy the devil prowls around like a roaring lion looking for someone to devour."

Do you ever just want to know what God wants from you so you can do it already? I received a very clear call to ministry at 14 and then successfully wasted the next 10 years seduced by the devil trying to figure out what that meant for "me." I went through a stage desperately needing to be seen ministering to someone, anyone.

Humility is a funny thing. It often eludes us, prideful people. "You mean this really isn't all about me, Lord?" I had to write that one in my Bible, convinced God's Word to me was, "It's not about you." You might need to write it down as well. I often hear the retort of false humility when people say "I know it's not about me." Read that again carefully. Smell the deception. Who exactly is the subject of that sentence? Who is the first and the last? I distinctly remember God calling Himself the Alpha and

13

the Omega, the beginning and the end, the first and the last. Why then do we try to put ourselves in His rightful place? No wonder we have anxiety. We are trying to dethrone God with all the right motive we can muster. That is how the devil gets us…just like he did Eve. He convinces us of all the things we need to do and we do not rely on the Spirit to convict and control us. We have surrendered to the ebb and flow of something entirely different.

Prayer is our weapon. The Word of God is our guide, our true north.

Pray asking God to reveal any false humility in you. If you tell Him of your need for an authentic, humble, spiritual witness, don't think He won't meet your very real need. He is the God who always has a ram in the thicket for any heart that truly desires His will even when it isn't clearly understood.

Protect yourself with the true revealing Spirit of Christ. He alone bears witness to His perfect nature. He will let you know if what you believe is truth. Ask Him.

My prayer is that you will pray for and attain a teachable spirit, protection, and Godly wisdom.

Chick Tip of the Day

Do: Take a nap

Don't: Take a nap if you are at work, driving, or have a 2 year old on the loose.

DAY 5

2 Chronicles 29:30b

"They sang their praises with joy and reverence, kneeling in worship."

My husband Denbigh (den bee) was called to lead worship many years ago and has been faithfully serving God through many financially rough patches. I am constantly amazed at how the Spirit ministers to him and turns God's Word into lyrical genius. It can seem like you know everything and have it down when you do four to five services at different venues every week. I will tell you we are always learning about true, authentic worship.

Backtracking a bit, I grew up being taught to be quiet in church. People in my church thought that people raising hands was "creepy." I think the fact was that these people were desperately afraid of the all-encompassing power of the Holy Spirit. When I saw people worshiping God in complete abandonment I knew I wanted that for myself. I sought out to experience God like that. It wasn't until a time of great hardship that I experienced God in that way. It is so easy to get numb to the Spirit and just sing to God. Being aware of this, something aroused my awareness recently. It is a tiny book by Robbie Castleman called "Parenting in the Pew." It is a book to teach your children how to worship. Let me tell you what girls, God put a Word in there for me. I needed to put the worship back in the worship service! Me. "The worship pastor's wife." I wasn't aching to be filled with the spiritual presence of God. (Oh, if this got out!) This has caused some serious reflection on my part. Was I singing too much and not saying anything? Was I worried about my appearance or if people were hearing me? I would move to the back during worship and now I sing to one man unhindered.

I pray you the grace and favor to worship Christ in Spirit. May you see everything you serve more readily than Him. God, give this tender woman the fruits of worshiping you. May His joy be in you.

"Clear the stage. Set the sound and lights ablaze if that's the measure you must take to crush the idols." Ross King

Chick Tip of the Day

Do: Have yourself a worship service in your living room.
Don't: Forget to relinquish control to the Spirit of God to move you.
Suggested Worship: Nichole Nordeman, Derek Webb, David Crowder, Ross King

DAY 6

2 Kings 20:5b

"I have heard your prayer, I have seen your tears; behold, I will heal you."

Wow! Say this out loud. "God has heard my prayer. God has seen my tears. GOD will heal me."

I don't know where you are today, but I can guarantee some part of you feels just a bit broken. "Why can't I get past this, Lord? How am I supposed to love this person when they act his way? Why can't I overcome this sin?" In the famous words of parents everywhere, "You just can't." That's true. No prescription. No anecdote. No program. By your power you cannot fix anything.

I have, for as long as I can remember, been at odds with my mother. Our personalities are immeasurably different. We don't deal with things the same. She is abrupt and can hurt those she is trying to help with her words. I am straightforward but tender. I can't tell you how many times that I have tried to fix it and she has tried to control it... each in our own horrible way. You could guess that it never worked. We were always in turmoil.

It got to the point that I finally broke down to God, repented and confessed that I couldn't do it anymore.

You will never guess what God did. I don't live in a fairy tale, but I am friends with my mom. I never thought I would be able to say that. The amazing thing is how He went about it. I was sure that He would fix it by making her all better. He changed me. He made me less sensitive to her remarks by filling me and making me more supernaturally aware of His love.

When we are full of God we don't need much from anyone else. It's all overflow. Let me tell you when you feel drip dry nothing feels better than overflow. God's love is a wellspring that flows into everything we are. Who knew? God's love changed me.

Thank you for the humility, Lord.

Weep at His feet today knowing He will hear and heal you.

"I am the Lord who heals you." Exodus 15:26

Chick Tip of the Day

Do: Plant something. Growing things is a gift to yourself.
Don't: Kill what you planted. (Good spiritual advice in that as well)

DAY 7

Haggai 2:5

"My Spirit is in your midst; do not fear."

I encourage you to read Haggai. It is only two chapters. There is a call to you there. It is a call to build up God's house. In verses four and nine of chapter one He specifically rebukes His people for building up their own houses while God's house laid in ruins. These people didn't understand why they were getting so little from so much labor. (Ever felt like that?) This nation had a calling much as we do to build the church. Yet, their land was unclean from idol worship and no attempt had been made at cleansing. They needed so much to complete the task and had so little. And God said, "My Spirit is abiding in your midst; do not fear." I just picture a room of little children overwhelmed by a large task and God, their teacher, saying, "Don't worry about the bullies. I know we are short on glue, but people will bring us even more than we can use requiring nothing in return. Let's get rid of everything that is dirty and clean up. We will do this together." God, the greatest teacher, always meets our simplest needs.

Let me ask you a personal question. Is there something in your house that is unclean or unpleasing to God? A little after Denbigh and I were married I started to understand all that God considered unclean in our lives. Huge garbage bags of stuff left our home. My husband who was a pack rat had a hard time letting go of stuff.

Ask God to reveal these things in your life. What is robbing you of blessing? Throw it out. Give yourself over to God and open wide the storehouse of your heart. God's love is going to overflow.

Now I know Christians are supposed to pray all the time. I also know that we don't. The sad statistic is that some 75% of the Christian church have never read the Bible in it's entirety. So I want to suggest something to you that seems simple, but obviously isn't. Commit to learning God's statutes for your life by reading His Word. Pray a prayer of dedication and cleansing in your home. If you are saucy, make it party- invite friends over to pray and eat hors d'oeuvres. Never had a prayer party? Neither had I, until I became desperate for God's blessing. It has changed my life. Remember, God wants to help you with everything. God is saying to you, "We will do this together."

Dig deeper: "Lord, I want to be whole" by Stormie Omartian

Chick Tip of the Day

Do: Throw out Cosmopolitan magazine. God designed sex. Don't you think He can help a married woman be wildly creative with her husband? Ask Him. Read Song of Solomon. Tommy Nelson did a great study on this.

Don't: Forget to pray for a passionate, desperate desire for you and your mate towards each other.

DAY 8

1 Thessalonians 5:19-21

"Do not quench the Spirit; do not despise prophetic utterances. But examine everything carefully; hold fast to that which is good."

God held a plumb line against His people in the Old Testament to measure them against His goodness. As you can guess they wavered from God's perfection immeasurably. Since it took me a minute to grasp this concept I will share the simple truth that I learned. A plumb line is a long string weighted at one end to determine true vertical values, a straight line. Your true vertical value is Christ. Our ideas of value and of goodness are so far removed from God's. Often Old Testament people were completely oblivious to their sin. They did it boldly in God's house and called it sacrifice. There was sex with temple prostitutes. The Pharisees led God's people with lies, deception, and murder. Isn't that insane? Yet, when I put God's plumb line against my life I see the same desperately evil stories. I wasn't in the Word every day and I couldn't discern God's voice. Believe me, there are many voices that will try to convince you that they are God. They are always easy to follow and lead to sin. Sin quenches the Spirit. It makes you unable to hear and thus operate in God's will. God's Word is the only thing you have to measure your life up with God's will. It is what you use to understand and discern the truth of the nature of God's goodness.

It is in no way easy or natural to be in the Word every day. Pray. Pray. God can equip you and draw you far beyond anything you can do in your own power. Let Him.

What are you measuring your life by with now? Is it your mother's opinion? Is it pressure you feel from people in your office, school or church? Who are you comparing yourself to?

Don't envy anyone who seems to have more than you.... even godliness. Know God is sovereign and in complete control of who you are.

Let God's will be your plumb line.

Sweet Jesus, make us aware of the truth of your goodness.

Chick Tip of the Day:

Do: Find a few minutes of solitude. It is the greatest gift you can give yourself.

Don't: Forget to linger at His feet today.

..."The enlargement of the heart compriseth the enlightening of the understanding. There arises a clearer light there to discern spiritual things in a more spiritual manner; to see the vast differences betwixt the vain things the world goes after and the true solid delight that is in the way of God's commandments; to know the false blush of the pleasures of sin and what deformity is under that painted mask and not be allured by it; to have enlarged apprehensions of God, His Excellency and greatness and goodness; how worthy He is to be obeyed and served; that is the great dignity and happiness of the soul; all other pretensions are low and poor in respect of this. Here then is enlargement to see the purity and beauty of His law, how just and reasonable, yea, how pleasant and amiable it is; that His commandments are not grievous, that they are beds of spices; the more we walk in them, still the more of their fragrant smell and sweetness we find.." Robert Leighton

DAY 9

Hebrews 10: 24-25

"And let us consider how to stimulate one another to love and good deeds, not forsaking our own assembling together, as is the habit of some, but encouraging one another; and all the more as you see the day drawing near." Hebrews 10: 24-25

Who have you loved and stimulated to good deeds lately? It sounds a little over- whelming if you ask me. I tried to do it a few times. It didn't work. I would busily write notes and call people to try to encourage them to be more than they were. Let me just tell you that if you are thinking of doing this, think again. We make poor versions of the Holy Spirit.

Since then I have discovered something amazing. Living, truly living your life is a powerful thing. The key has been in praying for the supernatural ability to genuinely love people and life. It was completely unnatural to me. My concept of love was distorted. Now I enjoy people. God has blessed me with a deep desire to transcend the temporal and seek godly intimacy with people. God uses me to meet the real needs of people and not the superficial wants I was placating.

I pray you each of you at least one intimate girlfriend; one chick that keeps it real and draws out your wild passionate love of life. I love my girlfriends.

Being one who was once afraid to go to her mailbox or be seen for who she truly is, this is a God-thing and it's exciting! I always felt like this crazy woman in a red convertible lived deep inside of me, but I kept her stuffed in a neat box. No one could ever see her under my cute, conservative, safe sweater set.

I want to encourage you to live out loud. As Mark Buchanan says live "unsafe." One fun thing I did was go to a vineyard with my girlfriend, Suzi. (Did all the Baptists just gasp?) Really, we share a desire to see all the things Jesus spoke of in His word. We also got to stomp a few grapes "I Love Lucy" style.

So, take a pottery class. Go to a petting zoo. Ask God to show you His wonders.

Ask God to reveal some beautiful qualities and vulnerabilities in a friend. Encourage her to sing, dance, write, and live out the wild life of abandonment Christ has called her to. Live it with her. Dance in parking lots. Sing a song from "The Sound of Music" while waiting in line at an Italian restaurant. She will be spurred on, as will you.

Chick Tip of the Day:

Do: Paint an original piece at one of those paint your own ceramic stores.

Don't: Go alone.

DAY 10

1 Corinthians 2: 9-10

'But just as it is written, "Things which eye has not seen and ear has not heard, and which have not entered the heart of man, all that God has prepared for those who love Him." For to us God revealed them through the Spirit; for the Spirit searches things, even the depths of God.'

Are you more afraid of the Holy Spirit than you are the enemy? I suggest to you that is natural. Of the two the Holy Spirit is definitely the most fearsome, but He is also the only good. The problem is that we surrender to the fear of the enemy and run from the fear of God.

Have you ever been around people who just love the Holy Spirit? I am one of those. I just love to watch Him do His thing! I love to pray. I love people who love to pray. There is something accomplished when we pray that goes far beyond what we can see.I find myself asking God for a glimpse of what He is doing. I love what Moses said in Exodus 33:18, "…I beseech you, show me your glory." I get a rush from that. I know that we do not see much of what God is doing because we do not ask to see it. I pray you eyes to see today my sisters! Why not get on the glory train and praise Him!

You can see more than you do now. I know. I lived many years of my life with a veil clouding my vision and my theology. One of the greatest things I discovered in the Word of God was the long line of promises. In James 5:16 it says that if we pray for others we will be healed. I experienced that. I knew why I was being healed and I gloried in my Creator!

Dig into the meat of the Scripture, claim every promise, and praise Him upon delivery. Praise Him! He will deliver. I love how it says He will deliver in Ephesians 3:20, "…do abundantly, far over and above all that we [dare] ask or think [infinitely beyond our highest prayers, desires, thoughts, hopes, or dreams]" He does that abundant action by His power that is at work in us, His Holy Spirit. I feel like shouting "Amen!"

Ask the Spirit to search you today. Ask for personal revelation of where He is working in your life. I am praying for you to experience that awesome power this moment. Is there something in your life that you need to see God's glory in? I am praying that for you right now. May you see God reveal Himself in that situation. May you worship Him as you never have before. May you experience the abandon that accompanies the Spirit filled life. That is the blessing I have asked God to give you as you read this. I pray you teachability and the openness to receive everything the Spirit desires to offer you. I love you deeply.

Chick Tip of the Day

Do: Pray as David did in Psalm 139:23 "Search me, O God, and know my heart; test me and know my anxious thoughts."
Don't: Wear royal blue eye shadow, no matter how many people tell you it looks nice.

DAY 11

Zachariah 2:5

"For I declares the Lord, will be a wall of fire around her, and I will be glory in her midst."

Zachariah 4:6

"Not by my might nor by power, but by spirit says the Lord of hosts."

On our honeymoon, Denbigh and I went to Cancun. One day, we were playing on the beach and decided to run into the ocean. Denbigh did just fine. I, on the other hand, looked sadly like a goofy cartoon. I was knocked down with every step I took. I would try to blame it on the height of the wave, but it wasn't even at my waist. I was being pulled down to a mouthful of sand by the undercurrent going out.

That is what the Holy Spirit is about. He is a powerful force whose main goal is to make us realize we can't stand on our own two feet. We often find ourselves looking at the surface level blaming the foot high waves for our woes, for things being moved out of our perfect order. The reality is that God isn't about the surface level. He isn't about the surface level that will pass away (though He is concerned about all things).

God is about the heart. The undercurrent of the Holy Spirit is working in ways unimaginable to us as we stare at the surface. I wondered what would happen if I just lay down with my head under the water. Naturally, I would see and be moved by the undercurrent. I would not be focused on the surface. I would be released to the ebb and flow of the Spirit of God. Can you imagine? What if you were completely lost in the current, completely submissive to the way of the water? Would you be out of control? Yes, and praise Jesus! That is what He is calling you to. He accomplishes all things in this world by His Spirit.

If we know Him we can see what those things are. There are simple things we can do to release ourselves to His work.

I once heard a woman in my Bible Study Fellowship class talk about how God told her to recognize where He is working. She home schools her kids and keeps their homework in a three ring binder. Every time they punch holes they apply page protectors to them. That is where the Spirit spoke to her. He simply asked what she was using to reinforce her relationship with Him. Every time we read the Bible, do a Bible study, fellowship, worship, pray, or read about Him we reinforce our relationship. Those reinforcements keep us in our place. We are not easily torn away from the place God ordained for us from the beginning of time.

Ask Him to give you the gift of drawing near to Him in every aspect I described. Ask to see where He is working. Ask for divine appointments to work with Him becoming the active gospel in the lives of people. Be intimate with Him, relishing every gift He gives you.

"The Holy Spirit is the gift." –Henry Blackaby

Chick Tip of the Day

Do: deep condition
Don't die your hair some crazy color!

DAY 12

Galatians 5:25-26

"If we live by the Spirit, let us walk by the Spirit, let us not become boastful, challenging one another, envying one another."

I am ready for a raised eyebrow on this one. In driving to a camp where my husband was leading worship, I ran across an old song on the radio. It was Jeanie C Riley singing Harper Valley PTA. This song is horrible and hilarious. It is a song about a small-town PTA group attacking a woman because they did not approve of how she dressed, the life she was living or how she was raising her child. This saucy woman proceeds to go down to their meeting to tell them that she knows how they are all living even though they perpetuate a façade of perfection.

After hearing this I called my husband and told him that I had an epiphany and that Jeanie C had brought me a word. (I can still hear his laughter) I went on to explain that I thought all church services should start by playing this song. He said, "Explain that one." I replied with an enthusiastic, "Husband, that is the same critical spirit that is ripping apart the female body of Christ.

Even some very godly friends of mine block the gift of intimacy with fellow believers by picking each other apart. Isn't it true, ladies? We are all on the prayer chain, but few of us are praying. I know it is tearing at God's heart. We shred our sisters to pieces because of outward appearance and external circumstance. Know this, sweet sister, from Genesis to Revelation, God calls it sin. God calls it sin.

John 7:24 says to quit judging by outward appearance and judge by what is right. God looks on the heart. What would He see if He looked on your heart right now? If you look on any fellow believer in Christ and concentrate on anything external, you should check your fruit. Criticism bears seedless, dead fruit.

I once had a minister try to tell me that I wasn't as godly because I wore mascara. He tried to explain that is what "He looks at the heart" meant to. Do you see that even this minister was operating in the flesh and that God does not operate in the flesh? God does not look on the appearance…not the make-up, but how things are, the mask we wear. He can gaze upon your heart and tell you who you are without ever gazing upon your face or checking your diploma wall.

You cannot love in your own power. Ours is the God who is. He offers us deep intimacy with our sweet sisters if we move beyond what is seen to what is unseen to seek their heart and His.

Chick Tip of the Day

Do: Engage in some fun exercise
Don't: Become heavy weight champion of the tri state area or reward your exercise with four candy bars!

Day 13

Jeremiah 13:27

> "As for your adulteries and your lustful neighings,
> The lewdness of your prostitution
> On the hills in the field,
> I have seen your abominations
> Woe to you, O Jerusalem!
> How long will you remain unclean?"

Who wants to read that! When is the last time you were excited to be called a dirty prostitute? I was moved beyond words when I discovered Derek Webb's song Wedding Dress right before my own wedding. The words are a bit hard core, but I think anything less would lose the meaning and the depth of our sin against God.

> …I am a whore I do confess
> But I put you on just like a wedding dress
> and I run down the aisle
> and I run down the aisle
> I'm a prodigal with no way home

but I put you on just like a ring of gold
and I run down the aisle to you
So could you love this bastard child
Though I don't trust you to provide
I am so easily satisfied
by the call of lovers so less wild
That I would take a little cash
Over your very flesh and blood...

Do you choose to wear the garments and not accept the call? Do you know the right words and act in piety? Do you think you have an intimate relationship with God? Do you know Him?

In the past few weeks I have heard an illustration so many times I knew I had to use it. People that are trained to spot counterfeit money never examine counterfeit money. They spend hours and hours examining the real thing and by doing so can easily recognize a bill that is not real. Are you real? Is God real to you? Do you form your opinion of who God is by listening to others? Do you ever seek Him out for yourself? Or are you one who is satisfied with lesser gods. Do you cling to a god who is safe and manageable? When will you be willing to lay down your sacrifice? Will you ever? Have you ever cried out to be broken to the point of full restoration or do you settle for the gravy of God's Word and never get into the meat? Chow down, my sisters. Don't be the one who does not get to experience Him in His fullness. Reach up. Bow down. Breathe in.

Chick Tip of the Day

Do: Go see a movie with a girlfriend
Don't: Forget to make it a girly one

DAY 14

2 Chronicles 15:7

"But you, be strong and do not lose courage, for there is reward for your work."

Did you know that Noah followed God's command to build a boat long before anyone had ever seen rain? Can you imagine? This boat is calculated to be 450 feet long, 75 feet wide, and 45 feet high. How long he must have worked on it before it even resembled the boat God said it would. No one can say for sure the amount of time that it took him, but the estimates are from 70 to 120 years! He died at 950 years old. That means that Noah spent close to a tenth of his life building this boat. What do you think was going through his mind all that time? When do you think he started to even see a vision for what God was ordering him to construct?

Have you been working at something for years and still aren't seeing the vision of what God has called you to? It often seems to work that way. God calls us and we expect to get to doing that thing full-time right away. Funny thing is that it doesn't work that way, hardly ever. We often run out and try to do it in our own power forgetting to inquire of our momentary steps from the One who called us. Are you still trying to be effective in your own power?

I once heard Christine Caine speak at a women's conference and something she talked about made sense to me. She told of her gift of speaking and how she must have come from the womb talking. People tried to convince her that she should leave her church and go where she would be utilized more. She didn't go though. She stayed under the headship of her pastor and simply served where she was. She said that he knew that the gift that was in her would over take her if she did not work out the blackness that was ruling her heart. Now she travels worldwide teaching hundreds of thousands of people.

God wants to do that in your life. It may feel like there are times when it seems that you will never attain the thing He has called you to. People will come against you and oppose your gift or they will idolize it and try to draw your focus to it. Focus on one thing, Christ. He is preparing you and equipping you for powerful service. The more you submit, the greater power you exercise in His name. Be faithful in the now moment with the people in your life and He will use you to do great things. He is your reward. May you see fruit from your labor today.

Chick Tips of the Day

One: Don't miss the boat.

Two: Remember that we are all in the same boat.

Three: Believe God. It wasn't raining when Noah built the Ark.

Four: Stay fit. When you're 600 years old, someone may ask you to do something really big.

Five: Don't listen to critics; just get on with the job that needs to be done.

Six: Travel in pairs.

DAY 15

Psalm 107:6 ,13, 19, 28)

Then they cried out to the LORD in their trouble;
He saved them out of their distresses.

Psalm 107:2

Let the redeemed of the LORD say so,
Whom He has redeemed from the hand of the adversary

Psalm 107:14

He brought them out of darkness and the shadow of death
And broke their bands apart.

Psalm 107:33

He changes rivers into a wilderness
And springs of water into a thirsty ground; Psalm 107:33

Psalm 107:20

He sent His word and healed them,
And delivered them from their destructions.

In the margin of my Bible, on a page in Corinthians, I wrote myself a note. It simply said, "He has already planned your release." Many times on the choice side of victory. Those words still intrigue me. For every sin I am trapped by, He has planned my release. No matter what I am dealing with, God is orchestrating the daily movement of my life for my good and His pleasure. If you have been trapped by depression that may seem like a hard thing to grasp. It is like being a wild animal being born into the captivity of a zoo. You know this isn't the life God created for you.

You feel completely alone. All you hear are the words of the enemy. Jesus endured that in the desert. Do you think He was tempted to not believe and waiver from full on confidence in God? Yes. The Bible says He has been tempted in every way. He was tempted by depression. All He had was the guidance of the Holy Spirit and belief that God's Word was accurate. Those are also your weapons against the work of the enemy. Know God. Study Him in Spirit and in Word.

Do you know the story of Hosea? God told him to marry a prostitute. She, as you might guess, went back to what she knew many times. Do you ever feel like that? In the end Hosea went and bought her out of slavery and put her back in her place, not as a slave, but as his wife. If you read the story you can feel the agony she must have been in, the shame the devil must have been holding her in. I often wonder what she was like after all her continuous trial with heritage and self. Who did Gomer become after she was redeemed by God through Hosea? She represents the redeemed in Christ. She must have become most excellent. She must have been righteous! I know from experience that God's healing is always better than life before the brokenness. Cling tight to His promise wherever you are. His healing is better.

..."I am the Lord who heals you." Exodus 15:23

Chick Tip of the Day

Do: Wash yourself in the water of the Word.
Don't: Spend another day without intimate study of the God you love.

DAY 16

Proverbs 3: 9-18

Honor the LORD with your wealth,
with the firstfruits of all your crops;
then your barns will be filled to overflowing,
and your vats will brim over with new wine.
My son, do not despise the LORD's discipline
and do not resent his rebuke,
because the LORD disciplines those he loves,
as a father the son he delights in.
Blessed is the man who finds wisdom,
the man who gains understanding,
for she is more profitable than silver
and yields better returns than gold.
She is more precious than rubies;
nothing you desire can compare with her.
She is a tree of life to those who embrace her;
those who lay hold of her will be blessed.

I once had a relative ask me why God allowed certain things
to happen. In this particular case this person was suffering from

an addiction to alcohol that led him to being arrested several times for assault, dui(s), public intoxication, and wrecking multiple cars while not holding a job for years. She was asking why God allowed him to keep in this cycle. I believe this man had submitted to the temptation of the enemy. In a way he chose it over God. He is at fault. God was simply trying to discipline him to get him to stop. She did not agree that God did these kinds of things. It says in His Word that He does. Hebrews 12:7 says, "It is for discipline that you endure; God deals with you as with sons; for what son is there whom his father does not discipline?"

That brings me to a question for you. How well do you know Him? Do you go on second hand knowledge of God? Do you think up what you believe Him to be like based on your idea of things? Do you withhold all you have in order to satisfy yourself? Do you disagree with the Bible as God's authority? Do you think it contradicts itself? Have you ever read it in it's entirety? Do you focus more on books about God than you do on His Word? My suggestion to you is to spend more time in the Source and less time in the exposition on the source. You should spend equal, if not more time, in the Word of God than you do in books about it.

I received a piece of mail from Kay Arthur's ministry today and on the front of the envelope it said, "Is Biblical Christianity disappearing?" Part of me knew the statistics that would be inside. Sad to say many people are substituting anything they feel for the truth of Christianity. We put ourselves on His throne and decide who we think He is and what we think He should be doing. We simply don't believe Him. In Matthew Chapter 7 it compares a Christian who knows the Word and goes back to his sinful lifestyle to a dog that returns to his own vomit and a clean pig that returns to the mire. Do you need an admonition to return and seek? In James it says let any man who lacks wisdom ask God for it. Ask Him right now. In Matthew it says ask and you will receive, seek and you will find, knock and the door will be open to you. Do you need an open door in your life right now? ASK Him. You have the mind of Christ if you are a Christian. Do not think that He doesn't want to fill you with the Spirit and knowledge of Him right now. I hear so many people say that they do not enjoy study. God can overcome that. The Bible comes in audio. It comes in many translations that are easy to read. I pray that you open yourself up to Him today.

Have you truly humbled yourself and told Him you know you are a sinner and there is no way to Heaven but by Him. Have you made Him Lord of your life? Do you need to put Him back on the throne of your heart today? Take a moment to do that right now. If you are able, get on your knees and praise Him.

Chick Tip of the Day

Do: Take a girlfriend to lunch (get the chicken salad).
Don't: Be a hermit.

DAY 17

-∰◯

2 Timothy 1:7

For God did not givve us a spirit of timidity (of cowardice, of craven and cringing and fawning fear), but [He has given us a spirit] of power and of love and of calm and well-balanced mind and discipline and self-control.

Isn't this a lesson we all need to know? It is a rare thing to find someone who is humble enough to be bold. I am not referring to people who are always saying things that rub people the wrong way or speak in a judgmental tone. I am referring to people who step out of their comfort zone to speak to people and exhort them on in the battle against their sin. We are afraid of our gifts.

We are afraid of our brothers and sisters in Christ. We are afraid of our anointing. In Ezekiel it clearly says that if we do not blow the trumpet and warn others about sin then we will be held accountable for their blood. Their blood will be on our hands. Why are we so afraid to operate in the power of our anointing? Pride.

CS Lewis says we are never more like the devil than when we are prideful. Pride rears its ugly head in many ways. To one woman it might be a haughty attitude and to another it might be a shy one. Why do we succumb to the fear of the enemy and refuse to operate in the power that has already been given to us? We always cooperate with the enemy and rebel against the calling on our lives.

The moment we believe and accept Jesus as our salvation we are anointed with the power of the Spirit of God. We are handed over every spiritual gift and yet they often go untapped and unopened. We cannot appropriate a gift that has not even been given a glance. It is like going into a battle with a sword that we have never wielded and in fact have not even removed from the sheath. It is pointless.

Where is the passion? Why are we content to wear a name and never do anything with what we have been given? I dare say it is because we do not know the God we claim to serve. We do not read His Word and we never attain an active prayer life. We allow ourselves to be redundant and become obsolete for the kingdom and then blame God for not using us. You cannot send people into battle when they leave their weapons in the display case at home. That will only usher in a lot of maimed or dead people. I love the picture in the Lord of the Rings when Aragorn starts acting as though he were a king. He restores his weapon. He wears it. He wields it with unmistakable precision. He is operating in the power and authority of who he is. He was king all along. Today I exhort you to do the same. Rebuke your adversary with the Word of God. Put on who you are in the Lord Jesus Christ and wield your weapon well. Do it and so become it. Claim every promise, every gift. It will radically change everyone around you.

Fear is the absence of faith.

1 John 2:20

"But you have an anointing from the Holy One, and all of you know the truth."

Chick Tip For the Day

Do: Play in the rain.
Don't: Play in hail.

Day 18

1 Peter 5:8

"Be of sober spirit, be on the alert. Your adversary, the devil, prowls around like a roaring lion, seeking someone to devour."

One thing I realize is that the devil hates life. Nancy Demoss will tell you that is why Satan loves abortion and homosexuality. He hates life in every form and will do everything he can to take it from you. I have come to find that he hates when we offer life through the Word as we minister to people. He also is the enemy of the pregnant woman. This may not apply to you, but please read on. It may be a word to someone you know.

The devil hates the pregnant woman. He hates that another soul can be offered the grace of God. If he cannot talk you into having an abortion, he will attempt to riddle your life with lies. One major thing I notice is not so much what is happening, but how we deal with it. A woman will probably come under more attack when pregnant than most any other time. We will have nightmares and suffer emotions we could not even dream of. We do not have to let it be our focus. We do not have to focus our attention on the nightmares and ignore the glorious miracle of God that is happening inside us. We must rebuke the enemy of life. Rebuke him with scripture and prayer.

We can ask God to equip us to even be fierce warriors in our dreams. Don't think He won't. One of the greatest things you can do for yourself the moment you know that you are pregnant is to find every praying sister that you can and be very real with them about all of your emotions, thoughts, and dreams. The power of prayer can keep you from letting your adversary steal away one of the most precious times you will ever experience. Do not let him. Claim these life giving moments in the name of the Lord Jesus. Praise Him.

The Bible says that He inhabits the praise of His people. Praise is a powerful thing. It invites Him into the thing you are dealing with. It says that you trust Him with it. Give it to Him. Tell God that you do not understand and that you cannot deal with it on your own. Tell Him that you need Him to be in control of this. He is and He will. He is already working it out for your good. He has already planned your release. He just needs you to see and know that.

The battle is won and lost in the mind. In reality the battle is won. The devil tries to convince you otherwise. He reminds you of every shortcoming, sin, every abortion. You, however, are not those things. You are clean. God loves you enough to let you experience life inside you. His desire is that you experience life to the full.

Today, you have the mind of Christ. The mind of Christ is steady and unyielding to temptation. Bear witness to the heart of God in that mind. Ask for protection of that mind. I pray that you fully operate in the mind of Christ. I pray you godly women to surround you and I pray blessings, protection, and clarity over you. May you experience every joyful moment and focus on it. Remember that the devil hates for things to work as God purposed them. He hates sex in the confines of marriage and the fruit of the womb. Stand firm against him and live out godly purposes.

Chick Tip of the Day

Do: Get yourself in a prayer group
Don't: Neglect taking care of yourself

DAY 19

⌘

1 John 4:1

"[Test the Spirits] Dear friends, do not believe every spirit, but test the spirits to see whether they are from God, because many false prophets have gone out into the world."

When did we as Christians stop testing the spirits? Most of the people I know are listening to word-faith teachers and eating up the prosperity doctrine. We are basing our church models on men who are heretical. Sometimes I find myself wanting to scream out! Can't we stop wanting to be entertained and immerse ourselves in the power of the Word of God. Sadly, even in our walk with Christ we are often in it solely for what is in it for us. We want a better life, better kids, better stuff. We want better churches, with better programs so we can benefit. We do not question David Cho, Joel Osteen, or Joyce Meyers if they show us the path to what we want. Sure there is plenty of good teaching mixed in and so we excuse the lack of sound Biblical doctrine.

Whenever Christ would encounter a demon in the New Testament the demon always proclaimed Him to be Christ. There was always truth told by the demon and mingled somewhere in there was a lie. There was always something slightly off to distract from the truth or the Deity. It is the same today. They proclaim God to be God or Christ to be Christ. [The lie is hidden somewhere in their teaching.] Some will tell you that Christ obtained our salvation in hell. Some will heal you for money. Some make a spectacle of the wonders of God. Some say name it and claim it.

Where do we find the truth? We measure everything by the Word of God. We pray for discernment. Be wary of what is popular. Seek godly counsel and apologetics indexes. Stand firm against anything that isn't fully the truth. The true Word of God is often found in small places, through narrow doors. It is a rare find. It is unadulterated and pure. It isn't about showing you the way to build up anything but the kingdom of God.

Chick Tip of the Day

Do: Pray for discernment and strength for your pastor
Don't: Be swayed by anything that detracts from the truth

Day 20

Psalm 73:25-26

"Whom have I in heaven but You? And I have no delight or desire on earth besides You.

My flesh and my heart may fail, but God is the Rock and firm Strength of my heart and my Portion forever."

Psalm 5:11

"But let all those who take refuge and put their trust in You rejoice; let them ever sing and shout for joy, because You make a covering over them and defend them; let those also who love Your name be joyful in You and be in high spirits."

I sit here asking God if there is a word He would have me say. All I can hear is "Delight yourself in Me." I close my eyes and breathe in the wonder of all I know to be true of Him. God, you amaze me. Your love is extravagant. I cannot stop singing that. I do not have a desire or delight besides You. As you have made it clear that I (mankind) am the chief end of all you are doing here, so I pray that You are the chief end of all that I do.

How I cry out to submit to Your will like the birds naturally migrate. Move me like the ebb and flow of the ocean. Allow us to be submerged and given over to Your will. Let us delight in you. May we taste you and know that You are all we long for. We praise You that You are our strength even when we cannot go on. You do not fail us. You do not fail. Oh God, that we would embrace You as our portion as the psalmist has. May we have no other claim or want besides You. Lord God, anoint our lips with your praise that we may experience Your inhabitance. Let us see Your glory! Open our eyes. Give us ears to hear. Do not leave us a deaf and dumb people who cannot fathom a need of You. Let us worship you experientially. We do not long to give you lip service, God. We long to see and experience the pleasure and glory of the incarnate Word, the living One. Reveal Yourself to us. Change us into new people who magnify Your name. Make us people you delight in. Form us into people that bless You and give You pleasure. Give us the great gift of calling on Your name for refuge! You are our most precious and righteous covering. Give us unspeakable joy in all that You are. We love that You are. Anything we long for desperately we know that You say, "I am." You are that You are that You are, Lord. We are thankful. We praise Your holy name. Let us not only see but also experience who You are. Draw us deep into Your character and Your word. May we drink deep and taste all the sweetness you offer us. May we give you enough room in our lives for the entire blessing you desire to give us. May we love You. Even that is a gift you give. I ask it for every person who reads this. May each one be drawn into the secret and exquisite nature of Your love. Be blessed. We love and celebrate You.

1 Chronicles 29:11

"Yours, O LORD, is the greatness and the power and the glory and the victory and the majesty, indeed everything that is in the heavens and the earth; Yours is the dominion, O LORD, and You exalt Yourself as head over all."

Chick Tip of the Day

Do: Take a day off for yourself.
Don't: Spend it watching television.

DAY 21

Isaiah 53:4-6

"Yet it was our weaknesses he carried; it was our sorrows that weighed him down. And we thought his troubles were a punishment from God for his own sins! But he was wounded and crushed for our sins. He was beaten that we might have peace. He was whipped, and we were healed! All of us have strayed away like sheep. We have left God's paths to follow our own. Yet the LORD laid on him the guilt and sins of us all."

Do you ever look around you and wonder where the fire is? Where is the passion that burned so vehemently in the prophets and apostles? One Sunday staring into the empty faces of the members of my church I found myself asking God that very question. Where is the fire?

God clearly said to me that the fire I longed to see in my fellow Christians was and is a product of suffering. We are a people who do not allow ourselves to suffer. We feel inclined to prevent the onset of suffering by getting what we believe we deserve. Mostly, we believe that we don't deserve what we are getting, and we do not deserve to be treated in a particular way. We over medicate ourselves and our children. We over eat. We over indulge. We shop until we can't pay our bills and live buried in debt. We fornicate and procreate with all the wrong motives. We miss the fruit that comes from allowing ourselves to endure trial. We miss out on uttering one of the most powerful prayers there is.

That prayer is when you cry out to God and say I cannot do this. We miss out on feeling that our sin is forgiven because we refuse to take ownership of it. We will not admit that it is our sin that crucified Christ and so we cannot accept His forgiveness and grace. We place blame on everyone but ourselves. We even place the blame on God. We do not trust in His character. We question what He does and does not do in life and in Scripture.

If He allows death or destruction we say He isn't good. We devalue the sacrifice. We refuse the gift. We do not receive the Spirit. We hide our faces from any one who would seek to confront us. WE are easily offended! Where does the offense truly lie? It lies in our black hearts. It lies in our bitter actions toward our "friends." When someone does not treat us as we deem we deserve, we cut that person out of our lives. Our covenant God acts that way only toward sin.

There are so many things in the Old Testament that we don't understand. Why did He kill babies or allow them killed? Why were people "smote" for making a mistake? It was an example to us to radically amputate our sin. What do we do with that example? We spit in the face of Christ and refuse His work in our lives. We refuse to suffer for His namesake. We know we are called to suffer and yet we cannot understand it when it comes.

How do we become one who carries the flame? We take inventory of our sin. We accept that WE are responsible for it and no one else. We cry out to God from the pit of despair. We listen and appropriate His Word to us. We know His character.

Chick Tip of the Day

Do: Rest in Psalm 4.
Don't: Try to doctor your own wounds.

Day 22

1 Corinthians 2:5

"So that your faith might not rest in the wisdom of men (human philosophy), but in the power of God."

I love the fact that our faithfulness does not rely on our own ability to have and maintain faith. He who called us is faithful. It amazes me that God is everything! We cannot do enough or be enough to try to be anything to Him. Sit back, abide, and it all just happens on it's own. It's unfathomable really. It is no wonder so many religious doctrines focus on us doing for God. How could He love us otherwise? The truth is that He does love us. God alone is faithful. God alone is love. The only way we can even attempt to get our minds around the infinitude of the attributes of Christ is through relationship with Him.

Some neighbors of mine live a very regimented religious life and they claim to serve Jesus. You cannot see it reflected in their lifestyle or their speech though. As Dan Schaeffer puts it, "they're faking church." Sometimes I just want to jump up and down and scream, "He just wants to love you." We all get trapped by rules though—either in keeping them or breaking them.

There is only one thing you can know. Jesus Christ is the Son of God, Lord of all the earth and He desires for you to know Him intimately. He knows everything about you. He numbered the hairs on your head, remember?

When is the last time you sought God first hand? It is so easy to pick up a book about Him, but when is the last time you sat alone and cried out "Reveal yourself to me"? A.W. Tozer says that anyone of any religious faith can call out to the ONE TRUE GOD and He is faithful to answer. No matter where you are or who you perceive Him to be, He is faithful to answer. If you are Mormon, Muslim, or Protestant, call on the name of the only God of Heaven and Earth. Be ready. Be open. Be teachable. He will blow your mind with His truth (not our version of it). May you be drawn to always believe and know who He really is.

Chick Tip of the Day

Do: Buy some fabulous lotion and use it every day.
Don't: Forget to rub it all the way in before you leave the house.

Day 23

Ephesians 5:33

"...And the wife must respect her husband."

I once heard a dear friend talking about how she did not enjoy sex with her husband on occasion. She would just lay there and hope he would get it over soon. That burdened my heart in such a way that I cannot explain. I was sad at how she was dishonoring her husband by telling other women how she often finds him undesirable.

I find that this is a common epidemic in our culture. We all tell our girlfriends how our men are lacking. We complain to each other. We laugh about it together. We dishonor and disrespect our mate. We lean on each other and chalk up our musings to hormones. Hormones or not, it is sin. It's a lie we have bought into and convince ourselves it's okay. It is not okay.

If we are complaining about our mate at all, we are living outside the guidelines God has gifted us with. If you have a girlfriend that listens, gives godly counsel, and prays with you that is a different story. We often confuse confidant and counselor. If your girlfriend is agreeing with you and can't believe your man is acting that way, you probably are not receiving counsel. The thing God's Word says you need to focus on is you. Pray with your friend about how you can be a better wife to encourage change and growth in your husband. Pray that your own heart will be right. Be obedient to the Word of God. Be respectful of your husband in every situation, with every word.

Discontent breeds a host of things that are nasty like infidelity and hate. Be wary of friends who agree with your bad report. Sin is deadly when it has the fuel of someone agreeing with and affirming it. I have a friend who did not like another friend's husband because all she ever heard was how this woman was treated badly and her husband didn't support her. She was telling me these things so I would get on the bandwagon against him. I told her she was a bad friend who was encouraging sin and disobedience to the will of God for this woman's marriage.

Are you encouraging a friend to sin and disobedience? Are you gathering support for your own refusal to submit and respect? Do you honor your mate and others with your words and actions? I pray each of you the desire to be a godly wife of godly means. I pray you deep respect for the integrity of your husband. May you never make a mockery of him in front of others.

Chick Tip of the Day
Do: Clothe yourself in humility and respect
Don't: Forget the rest of your clothes!

DAY 24

2 Corinthians 11:2

"I am jealous for you with the jealousy of God himself. For I promised you as a pure bride to one husband, Christ."

I do not understand others sometimes. How can we go in and hear the most moving sermon and fail to apply it to our lives? We leave the building to dishonor each other and provoke wrath and ruin. I dare say we spend the sermon thinking of how this fits so many other people's lives and how they need to hear this word. We might be so focused on filling in the blanks that we miss His message. The message is simply this…He wants you. You are a sinner. He desires to clean you. You must lay down your pride and humble your spirit. He is jealous to change you.

Unless God is giving you a Word to exhort a fellow believer, resist trying to fit the sermon to them. It is okay to think about yourself. Think of how you can be a better daughter, wife, mother, friend. Do not let the devil make you focus on how you are not these things. Do what God's Word says: Get busy doing!

How can you serve and honor the people around you? How can you serve and minister to God by touching the lives in your life? How can you wash your sisters with the pure water of the Word?

We are here to clean and keep cleaning our sisters, knowing that God is jealous for us all. He desires us to have godly jealousy toward each other. If you see sin in someone's life confront it. Leave the rest to God. I love that He says He will rebuild the former devastations in Isaiah 61. That means it is up to Him. We don't have to mount a building campaign or try to figure it out for ourselves. He will do the thing. He is doing it. All we need to know and keep knowing is relationship. That relationship is a gift. We need to thank the Lord Jesus and ask for more and more. Pray intimacy for yourself and everyone you know. The heart knowledge is vital. Most of all believe on Christ who is your righteousness and purity. He is faithful to keep you clean. Let Him.

Ask yourself if you are dishonoring a loved one with your speech or actions.

How could you remove this hindrance to intimacy with God? In honoring Him you naturally honor others. If you are not honoring others there is something that needs to be evaluated in your relationship with God. Do not be a person God gave eyes and ears to but refuse to see or hear. Ask Him if you are dishonoring Him. He is jealous for your full restoration.

Chick Tip of the Day

Do: Go see a play
Don't: Forget to laugh at life's idiosyncrasies

DAY 25

⟨ornament⟩

John 10:10

"The thief comes only in order to steal and kill and destroy. I came that they may have and enjoy life, and have it in abundance (to the full, till it overflows)."

I once heard about an experiment that was performed on psychiatric patients. The psychiatrists would overflow a sink and leave the water running. The patient is brought in and handed a mop. He is then told to fix the problem. The correct way is to obviously to turn off the faucet and then clean up the water. What most of the patients did was scurry to mop up the water never paying attention to where it was coming from.

I kind of laughed as I pictured it in my head. Then I heard the clear utterance of the Holy Spirit telling me that I do that very same thing every day. Ouch, Lord. I found that to be quite true though. I bet if you even mildly search you will find the very same thing that I did. I often clean and clean to try to fix things in my own power never once trying to wade through the water and meet my problem at the source.

If you are married, a parent, or have parents of your own I am sure you can relate. If you are alive, I bet you can relate. No amount of psychology, friendship, or even chocolate can help us like laying down our problems at the feet of Jesus. Stop putting band-aids on everything, Sisters! Deliver yourself to the healing one. Christ has overcome the world and everything in it. This is a spiritual war. When we try to fix everything in our own power and fight the devil with our own weapons its comparable to going to war with a cap gun. Remember this: You cannot use human weapons in a spiritual war.

The Indians used to throw flaming arrows to start fires to sidetrack their enemy with putting out fires so they could attack and kill them. Feel familiar? The book of Ephesians says that Satan tries to do the same thing to us. Ephesians 1:3 says we posses every spiritual gift and victory in Christ Jesus.

Though we cannot be eternally defeated, we can lay down everything Christ has given us to fight fires. Meet your problems at the source today.

By having the eyes of your heart flooded with light, so that you can know and understand the hope to which "He has called you, and how rich is His glorious inheritance in the saints (His set-apart ones)."

Ephesians 1:18

Chick Tip of the Day

Do: Buy a bright dress.
Don't: Compare yourself to others. God made each of our bodies unique and beautiful.

DAY 26

Mark 4:38-41

"But He [Himself] was in the stern [of the boat], asleep on the [leather] cushion; and they awoke Him and said to Him, Master, do You not care that we are perishing?

And He arose and rebuked the wind and said to the sea, Hush now! Be still (muzzled)! And the wind ceased (sank to rest as if exhausted by its beating) and there was [immediately] a great calm (a perfect peacefulness).

He said to them, Why are you so timid and fearful? How is it that you have no faith (no firmly relying trust)?

And they were filled with great awe and feared exceedingly and said one to another, Who then is this, that even wind and sea obey Him?"

How is it with so rich a Word and so powerful a God that we too have so little faith? Why are we so timid and fearful of the Gospel of Jesus Christ? I dare say it is because we do not know Him. We have not acquainted ourselves with His character and nature. We do not know our God. We decorate the small amount of knowledge that we do have to suit our own habits and lifestyle. We have a God that agrees with us or we have a God we are so afraid of that we cannot even speak to. Why do we try to play it so safe? If we don't know Him, we do not live out the authority He bestows to us as His children. We are people who are incessantly talking and never saying anything. We are like the disciples taken aback when we see the manifest power of God. It is available to us every day and yet we treat it like a novelty. Why do we scurry about and blame God as though He did not care? His perfect peacefulness is there for the asking.

How do you trust Him? A friend of mine would say, "just let go of the rope." You have no control. How do you see His power? Matthew chapter 5 states that those who hunger and thirst for righteousness will be filled. You will be full of His Holy Spirit, His righteousness. His Spirit is the key to seeing His power.

Are we afraid to see His manifest power in our lives because His power and authority would cause us to feel convicted of our sin? Yes. We are always afraid of the wrong things. I exhort you to cry out to God to see His marvelous presence in your life today.

Chick Tip of the Day

Do: Measure the weight of your words. Are you incessantly talking and not saying anything?
Don't: Neglect to meet with God each day.

DAY 27

Proverbs 27:17

"As iron sharpens iron, so one man sharpens another."

What does this mean to you? For many years I thought of it as some sweet, cute flower covered note making. We confuse little superficial comments with the reality of what this is. Once I was reading the verse and I wondered how metal grating off metal could be confused with sweetness. Have you ever heard a knife being sharpened? It is like fingernails being drug down a chalkboard. It is not pleasant. It is the Word that hurts. It convicts. It incites change. It causes greater faith. It is not the person saying you sing well or you gave a good talk. It's the person who challenges your sin and confronts the enemy of your life.

I looked up the Greek of all the words in the verse and thought I would share it here with you.

Iron: Tool, magnetic, strength, harshness, unpleasant, course, disagreeable to the senses (especially the sense of hearing), exacting
Sharpen: To be alert
Man: Champion, servant

One version uses the words:
<u>Countenance</u>: Faces, before and behind, in the face of, look or expression indicative of encouragement or moral support
<u>Friend</u>: Intimate, a person who is allied in a struggle or cause, one who supports a movement

Here is what I gleaned from that. You have a person who is allied in a struggle with you, the servant champion, who comes with something somewhat unpleasant to hear to make you alert to the schemes and traps of the devil that you may be facing.

Is there someone you are grating against? Know that you can keep rubbing in one spot, focusing on the thing you don't like about them, and knick their weapon or you can choose to sharpen their weapon with the Word of God, which is our sword. You have the opportunity to equip or rob your sister. "She said" and "she did" won't matter in eternity. God has given you this opportunity to purge and purify yourself. He has allowed hard situations to purify you. Trust Him. Sometimes God may even be sharpening you by allowing someone else to act the same way to you. Ask Him why. Rebuke the enemy of your life and your friend's life. Pray. Pray and submit to each other in such a way that brings conviction and healing to the body! It isn't meant to be easy to battle our flesh. Remember, in victory there is blessing. May the blessing that accompanies obedience be yours today.

Chick Tip of the Day:

Do: Grow a vegetable
Don't: Forget to ask God to grow it.

DAY 28

⁓⁂◯

Matthew 6:14

"For if you forgive people their trespasses [their reckless and willful sins, leaving them, letting them go, and giving up resentment], your heavenly Father will also forgive you."

How long are you going to let your bitterness rot you internally? How long will you continue to subject yourself to self-torture? If you hold onto a bitter root and refuse to forgive you needlessly give away power and self control. They control you. Do you disagree? Do you turn the other way when you see them coming? Do you act different when they are around? Does bitterness cause you to be a sinful gossip and a slanderer?

Are you so focused on yourself that you cannot allow the situation to heal? We are often so consumed with how things affect us that we forget that it is Christ who has bore the brunt of our sufferings. We tend to measure everyone by where we are (or think we are). I like a question I heard asked, "Are you the standard for everyone else you know?" I would have to say for too long I was. I did not like people who were not like me. You see, I thought I was the personified righteousness of Christ on earth. Needless to say that bubble burst (loudly). I realized that

I had probably never actually loved a person just like they were. I never loved God just like He is. I read in John 13:35 that they will know us by our love for each other and I wondered what I was known as since I did not have that. Obviously, I would not have been known as a disciple.

The Holy Spirit is so generous to give us things to pray when we find ourselves in a bleak pit of self-realization. He said, "Just ask Jesus to give you His heart for His Father."

That is when I found Matthew 5:3, "Blessed are the poor in Spirit for they will see the Kingdom of Heaven." There began my long trek to forgiveness.

How to forgive:

1. Ask God for humility. Humble people are not easily offended.
2. Ask God for the power of the Cross to heal your pain.
3. Ask God for focus. May you concentrate on the depth of the forgiveness you have received and the wicked way you may be operating in. Psalm 139:23
4. Ask to be made a peacemaker. Making the choice to forgive causes Satan to lose his foothold.
5. Ask God to give you a heart for the offender. (I know it's hard.)
6. Ask for pardoning and receiving for both of you. As you pardon your offender you are released from their power to hurt you. You will have restored intimacy with God. Blessings follow obedience.

Chick Tip of the Day

Do: Ask God for more joy than you can contain.
Don't: Wear a mask of hypocrisy to hide your unforgiveness.

DAY 29

—⚬—

Ephesians 6:2

"For our struggle is not against the flesh and blood, but against the rulers, against the authorities, against the powers of this dark world and against the spiritual forces of evil in the heavenly realm."

I have a lot to say about unforgiveness because it almost ruined my life.

When you set out to do anything that will plunder and invade the enemy's territory always ask God for protection and ask God to rebuke your enemy. You will be attacked with every kind of fear and every thought of failure. The forces of darkness will swarm around trying to re-seed every bitter root. Ask God to open your eyes to where the enemy is working and plans to work against you. Ask God to equip you for battle and teach you to wield your weaponry well. May you be fierce in your battle.

One of the most successful strategies of the enemy is to break the unity of the opposing force. Where is the division in your life? Submit that to God today. Remind yourself that He is our righteous judge and we should stand as the judge of no man. "Do not judge, or you too will be judged." (Matthew 7:1)

I looked up the Greek for the word judge in this verse and part of the definition was separate. If you deem one better than the other or yourself better than another and separate yourself from them it says that you will also be separate. If you separate yourself from others you are also separating yourself from God and the blessing of His intimacy. Isaiah 59:2, "But your iniquities have separated you from your God; your sins have hidden His face from you, so that He will not hear."

If you are in harms way with a certain person emotionally, mentally, physically, or spiritually ask God to help you determine appropriate boundaries. There is a way to keep healthy boundaries and still be salt and light to your offender.

Tell God the injustice or violation.

Release the emotions to Him.

Forgive each person for each hurt.

Forgive those who didn't protect you.

Ask for forgiveness for yourself for your own unforgiveness.

Chick Tip of the day

Do: Allow yourself some solitude today.

Don't: Forget to come back out.

Day 30

Job 42:10

After Job had prayed for his friends, the LORD made him prosperous again and gave him twice as much as he had before.

May I step on some toes today.

How are you dealing with how people treat you? Do you get mad and tell all of your other friends when people do you wrong? God doesn't make room in His Word for our self-righteous behavior. I looked long and hard at what all the friends and family of Job put this man through and how he dealt with it. I sometimes wonder why Job waited until chapter 42 to pray for his friends. I can almost see God saying, "Oh Job, just ask me to bless them and I will give it all back in abundance."

How often do you wait 42 chapters of life to pray for someone? Do you pray at all? Do you sit around discussing them and saying you doubt they will ever change? Are you crying out to God, "Help ME get through this"? How I long for the day we are all perfected, but am I praying for it? Am I praying for the people who speak harshly to me? Do I pray enough for a bitter in-law or do I get annoyed and talk about them? If something is pointed out to us, we are responsible for it. To whom much is given much will be required. Are you fulfilling your obligations? Or are you allowing your friends to stay in a pit and refusing them blessing? Are you refusing yourself blessing? Are you a gossip, a slanderer, a complainer? Quit working in step with our adversary.

Take a few moments to ask God to reveal to you who you are robbing of blessing and growth by resisting to obey God and pray for them. Write the names here if you need to.

Chick Tip of the Day

Do: some praise and worship right now!
Don't: Neglect your creativity.

DAY 31

"What I Tasted"

During a recent trip to a local bookstore something grabbed my attention. I saw a small elegant book entitled "What I Tasted: A Wine Lovers Journal." Those words drew me in and I decided to investigate the book. Inside were lines dedicated to when and where you tasted, the different ingredients depicted in each, how the bouquet smelled, type, year, type of barrel it was aged in, etc. Something about that seemed so passionate to me. Someone with this journal wanted to remember every aspect of a love they had.

As I was standing there a smile swept my face as I thought of recording my moments with God like that. How gracious He is. My moments could not fit in that little book. I have decided to try though and I invite you to do the same. Pick up a plain journal and write on it "What I Tasted: A God Lovers Journal." Record every moment you see His glory, how you felt, when and where. Look for what was tasted in Scripture. Here are some to get you started.

Psalm 34:8
Taste and see that the LORD is good; blessed is the man who takes refuge in him.

Psalm 119:103
How sweet are your words to my taste, sweeter than honey to my mouth!

Proverbs 27:7
He who is full loathes honey, but to the hungry even what is bitter tastes sweet.

Song of Solomon 2:3
[Beloved] Like an apple tree among the trees of the forest is my lover among the young men. I delight to sit in his shade, and his fruit is sweet to my taste.

Ezekiel 3:3
Then he said to me, "Son of man, eat this scroll I am giving you and fill your stomach with it." So I ate it, and it tasted as sweet as honey in my mouth.

Matthew 16:28
I tell you the truth, some who are standing here will not taste death before they see the Son of Man coming in his kingdom."

Luke 14:24
I tell you, not one of those men who were invited will get a taste of my banquet.' "

Hebrews 2:9
But we see Jesus, who was made a little lower than the an-gels, now crowned with glory and honor because he suffered

death, so that by the grace of God he might taste death for everyone.

Hebrews 6:4-5 For in the case of those who have once been enlightened and have tasted of the heavenly gift and have been made partakers of the Holy Spirit, and have tasted the good word of God and the powers of the age to come,

1 Peter 2:3 if you have tasted the kindness of the Lord.

May you crave all that will heal you today. May the righteousness of Christ be truth in your heart before it is uttered from your lips.

Chick Tip of the Day

Do: Make yourself a What I Tasted Journal
Don't: forget to tell Him how you feel about Him.

Day 32

Zechariah 11:11

"and so the afflicted of the flock who were watching me knew it was the word of the LORD."

A few weeks before I went to a Setting Captives Free conference I heard God singing a Norah Jones song to me over and over. When I finally was able to hear the song, it said, "Come away with me in the night and I will write you a song." On this page is that song. I was woken up with the first part at 4 am one night after learning the prophesy in the book of Zechariah above was about afflicted people being able to see and know Christ (the Word became flesh).

Struggling most of my life through deep affliction, this ministered to me. I often had hit the bottom, where I have been so broken in spirit that I could not even lift my head to worship my God. This song is my praise for getting to see and the result of my crying out for the gift of being able and allowed to worship God.

Râàh

(provide- to cause to see, trust, and enjoy God)

deep in the liquid darkness
where sound won't resonate
Your word is not as clear to me
I just can't feel your grace

but You have lovingly protected
all I willfully rejected
now I'm proud to be afflicted by this pain

hear me crying out from this place!!!

let me worship You, I beg of You, Father
anoint my lips with Your praise
it's only for Your glory–Your pleasure
may I see, trust and enjoy Your face

only the afflicted see the King
as we are perfected in our suffering

open my eyes to see You
enable my heart to trust You
open my mouth to taste You and enjoy

open wide my mouth and fill it

Psalm 3:3

But thou, O LORD, art a shield for me; my glory, and the
lifter up of mine head.

Chick Tip of the Day:

Do: Know that God sees you in your affliction.
Don't: Forget to ask Him to be the lifter of your head.

Thanks to Bible Study Fellowship, Beth Moore, and Keith Oglesby for loving the Word and inspiring me to dig deep into the Hebrew to better understand the scripture. May you be blessed with eyes to see and a desire to taste He who is good.

I recently found several references in Scripture to God giving songs in the night! See Job 35:10 and Isaiah 30:29.

Day 33

⦚

John 6:63

It is the Spirit Who gives life [He is the Life-giver]; the flesh conveys no benefit whatever [there is no profit in it]. The words (truths) that I have been speaking to you are spirit and life.

He gives everything!

One thing God has been teaching me during the past year is that He is the giver of everything. It is not exactly that He has chosen to give or take away something at a certain time. By Him everything is given or taken away. I like the Hebrew word for provide, Râàh. One of the meanings is to cause us to see. Oh how I beg for eyes to see for each of us! Everything He gives us is so precious and worthy of praise. Another similar word I like is Rô'eh from which Raah derived, means "shepherd" in Hebrew. A shepherd is one who feeds or leads his flock to pasture (Eze 34:11-15).One thing I daily thank God for is the ability to minister to other women. It is a sweet and delicate gift to work hand in hand with God to wash a sister in the water of the Word. How easy it is to write off someone who doesn't act "right" in our church setting. It is easy to point out why they act out or leave because we are studying the Word of God and they don't want to hear it. How often do we go after them and diligently pray for them? How often do we beg God for the gift of cleansing and sharpening our sisters? Not often enough. Right now, just thank Him for everything He allows you to do and every way He gives you to do it.

I wish I could put every reference to God giving or Him as giver in scripture. It is glorious! He is glorious!

He Gives:

Deuteronomy 20:14-plunder from our enemies
Job 32:8–understanding
Deuteronomy 12:10–rest and security from enemies
Deuteronomy 16:15–bountiful harvests and blesses work
Deuteronomy 32:39–life (and kills). He wounds and heals
Judges 8:7–victory!
1 Samuel 2:10-mighty strength
Job 5:10–rain
Job 5:11–prosperity to the humble
Job 33:4–life
Job 35:10-songs in the night
Job 36:6–justice to the afflicted
Psalm 41:2–prosperity
Psalm 68:6–joy

Job 36:6

He does not keep the wicked alive but gives the afflicted their rights.

Isaiah 30:20

Although the Lord gives you the bread of adversity and the water of affliction, your teachers will be hidden no more; with your own eyes you will see them.

Chick Tip of the Day

Do: Something you enjoy and thank God for letting you do it.
Don't: Focus on what you are not getting to do or do not have.

DAY 34

Matthew 3:11

"I baptize you with water for repentance. But after me will come one who is more powerful than I, whose sandals I am not fit to carry. He will baptize you with the Holy Spirit and with fire."

Lingering in the Living Water

I laughed probably out loud when I saw a woman sprawled out in a bath tub on the front of the program for a Ladies retreat I attended. I pictured her, much like myself, staying in there for a long time. I could hear the voice of my sweet country grandma from when I was young saying," If you stay in there any longer your hands are going to get pruny."

I can say to you that this retreat left much to be desired for me. It was so topical and superficial that I felt it had taken from the joy that I had. It made me ache for these women who needed to know more than how to cover a wound. We all needed healing. Don't think I am being over critical here. I promise you, I went there full of the Word. If you don't know what I mean, I hope you do by the end of this. I find that if you are daily eating the meat of God's Word that when you get to church and you go to retreat you are not looking to those things and people to fill and validate you. Maybe if the pew seems uncomfortable, I dare to say that it may not be the pew but how you are sitting in it. I believe I was positioned properly that day and looking forward to hearing the Spirit. He suggested to me that day of the idea of lingering in the Living Water. Pruny in the Spirit. God makes me laugh! I imagined women swelling up with Scripture. I want to tell you there is more to all of this. Don't abandon temporal things but invite God into them. He desires the best for you.

I looked up the word "pruny." I only found it in medical journals. In the dictionary the Lord opened my eyes up to prune: to cut back. In Bible Study Fellowship we learned that in John, when Jesus spoke of cutting off the dead branches he was not talking of throwing us in the fire, but removing from us the things that are unproductive in the Spirit." That's it, Lord!" That is what this book is about. It is a cutting away of things that keep us from the tasks that He foreordained for us.

Last week before I could start writing this book He made it quite clear to me that He wanted me to throw out all of my craft projects. I actually didn't fight Him. It felt really good to throw things out half done. I knew that they were merely filling up the time I could be doing what God desired of me. That is my suggestion to you. Throw out the things that have become a "have to get done." Who benefits? Does your spirit swell when you do them? Seriously, they will sell it from somewhere in China for cheaper than you can make it. Ask God what He created you for and pray to do it. Practice intimacy. One of my favorite songs written by Brett and Emily Mills is entitled Intimacy. Try learning it and praying it in song to God.

"Intimacy. I want to know you, Jesus, intimately. Apart from you I have nothing good. Hallelujah. I want to know you, Jesus. Hallelujah. You are my refuge, Abba. Hallelujah. You are my God."

Chick Tip of the Day

Do: Ask God to let you fill up with Scripture.
Don't: Blow up!

DAY 35

James 4:7

"Submit yourselves, then, to God. Resist the devil, and he will flee from you."

I remember thinking this was one of those things people say and no one ever does. "Oh you feel this way…you better resist the devil." How do you do that? You can simply say no to him. The question of how to actually make this applicable set me on a search to know how to "talk back to the devil" as AW Tozer puts it. It is a rare thing that the devil, himself shows up at your house and knocks on your door to hand you temptation. He does, however, constantly bombard our minds with lies. He usually puts them in first person, as though they are our thoughts, and waits for us to receive them and claim them as our own.

How do we resist a thought that sounds like one of our own? We dig deep into God's Word. Satan is not creative. God is creative. Satan keeps trying to use the same bait and the same lie over and over. How do we come against that? We know the truth and use it. Then if he makes us believe we are anxiety ridden or living in the sin of depression, focus on self, we can simply say, "no, in the mighty name of Jesus." Resist feelings

81

that do not seem right. Resist words that you do not feel are right. Do you ever start having thoughts about people that you aren't sure where they come from? " I can't believe she did that! She is so lazy, bossy, fat, selfish, etc." She may or may not be. It is not for us to side with the great accuser. It is ours to discern and intercede.

Funny thing, God's Word…it does not allow for an "if". It does not allow us to choose to forgive our father or mother "if they start acting right." Sometimes I hear people say that they have reason to feel a certain way toward people because of how they act, or acted 20 years ago, but that is a lie. As an adult who knows the Word of God, you are held accountable to it by Him. Even if the grace has to flow backward through your family line, so be it. Do not let the devil defile a godly legacy by believing him over obeying the commandments of Your God. He has a fresh Word for you here. Listen. What lie are you believing? Who do you have ungodly thoughts and actions toward? Are you leaving a legacy of the grace and active forgiveness of God?

May yours be a legacy that rewrites the pages of your family history. Saved. Saved. Saved. Forgiven. Sweet Lord, may it be.

Resist your enemy by the power of the Word of God. Know Scripture and rebuke the lie with the Truth.

Chick Tip of the Day

Do: Bake chocolate chip cookies.
Don't: Leave this day without asking God for the great gift of forgiving someone fully.

DAY 36

Ephesians 6:13

Therefore put on the full armor of God, so that when the day of evil comes, you may be able to stand your ground, and after you have done everything, to stand.

I have loved learning about Paul's meaning behind the armor more than most anything. As he was probably staring out of his jail cell at an armed guard God gave him yet another way we can operate in victory.

All of the things Paul mentions are Christ. In essence we are wearing Him. He forms Himself around us to protect us. I thought once that I could still be hit by the enemy in this armor and now I realize that I cannot. Don't get me wrong. God allows trials and tribulations to come into our lives. However, if we are safely wearing Him then the enemy who is trying to strike us actually strikes our Lord. We may feel the pain because of the Holy Spirit connecting us to Christ's pain. Every now and then I think we also try to stick a limb out just to get a battle scar to show people and make it all about us. Rest assured…it is about Him.

He is the Belt of Truth.
He is the Breastplate of Righteousness.
He is the Readiness of the Gospel of Peace.
He is the Shield of Faith.
He is the Helmet of Salvation.
He is the Sword of the Spirit…the Word of God.

As we find ourselves in battle we must focus on His wounds, by them we are healed. We must look to the cross of Jesus Christ.

We must not sit around simply praying on the armor. We must become intimate with the armor that is Christ. I pray that you seek to know each aspect of His character mentioned above. May He be all this to you. Operate in that faith. I love what God told Noah, "Now, leave the ark!" Walk away from your safe place today, fully ready for life and battle.

Galatians 3:27

For as many [of you] as were baptized into Christ [into a spiritual union and communion with Christ, the Anointed One, the Messiah] have put on (clothed yourselves with) Christ.

Romans 13:11-14

Besides this you know the time, that the hour has come for you to wake from sleep. For salvation is nearer to us now than when we first believed. The night is far gone; the day is at hand. So then let us cast off the works of darkness and put on the armor of light. Let us walk properly as in the daytime, not in orgies and drunkenness, not in sexual immorality and sensuality, not in quarreling and jealousy. But put on the Lord Jesus Christ, and make no provision for the flesh, to gratify its desires.

Chick Tip of the Day

Do: Go buy yourself the new book you've been wanting to read.

Don't: Paint any room in your house purple!

DAY 37

Philippians 1:14

And because of my imprisonment, many of the Christians here have gained confidence and become more bold in telling others about Christ.

Are you perhaps somewhere you never saw yourself being? Maybe yours are not prison walls. Perhaps they are. Are you so focused on your circumstance, finding that you are of no benefit to anyone? How are you acting where you are? Are you a hard worker? A good mother? A good mother-in-law? Do you spend the bulk of your time complaining about your situation or do you diligently try to live out the fullness Christ has for you there?

We complain in our homes, our jobs, our churches. I love something I heard Christine Caine say, "Even if you think your pastor is the anti-Christ, don't you think God is big enough?" He is big enough! Is your imprisonment inspiring people to work for the Gospel of Jesus Christ? Or are you fueling bitterness and resentment for authority figures in your life and the life of your co-workers? Do you talk poorly about your husband when he does not meet your expectations? Do you focus blame on how your children act when it comes to your attitude? The Bible says that YOU are responsible for your actions and attitude. You can pass no blame on the prison walls of your childhood, your marriage or your workspace. You are responsible for your sin.

Complaining is a sin. God has called us to be salt and light to people, all people. We all have to come to the same cross with the same amount of helplessness. Who are you hindering from seeing and embracing Christ because of your attitude? So your boss reminds you of Satan, does that stop the grace from flowing to him? Do you stop the grace from flowing to him?

Sometimes God puts people in our lives that seem unfair because we need to be confronted with a mirror image. When we were lost in the depth of our sin Christ died for us. Are you going that far for anyone? Do you look for opportunity to bless those who seem to curse you? What glory there could be if you led a depraved sinner to the throne of mercy and grace. Why do you starve those you deem as wicked and overfeed the kind? It's safe. It's easy. It guarantees that you do not have to grow in your walk.

It is time for an attitude check and a little prayer. Place your focus on Him who was afflicted for you. Live for Him right where you are. May God bless you there as He did Joseph who named his son Ephraim.

Genesis 41:52 He named the second Ephraim, "For," he said, "God has made me fruitful in the land of my affliction."

Ephesians 4:29

"Let no foul or polluting language, nor evil word nor un-wholesome or worthless talk [ever] come out of your mouth, but only such [speech] as is good and beneficial to the spiritual progress of others, as is fitting to the need and the occasion, that it may be a blessing and give grace (God's favor) to those who hear it."

Chick Tip of the Day

Do: Drink your favorite hot tea with honey.
Don't : Wear capri pants with high heels.

DAY 38

Psalm 3:8

"Salvation belongs to the LORD…"

Psalm 68:20

"God is to us a God of deliverances and salvation; and to God the Lord belongs escape from death [setting us free]."

I don't mean to sound harsh, but we are a truly arrogant people. Why do we think we can add to or take away anything from the cross of Jesus Christ? There is sin against an infinite God which requires an infinite sacrifice. How dare we believe we can add to and guarantee our salvation by what we do?

Some might ask how I could believe our salvation could not be lost. I say, "how could I believe otherwise?"

The sacrifice was perfect in every way. We are made into a new creature. Scripture never says we can revert back to the old creature. There are,however, examples given to say the opposite such as the vine and the branches in John 15. The Greek word there for cut off or severed is a word meaning that God delicately removes the fruitless parts. It is not indicative that God lops off a person. If you are brought to Christ and never mature and bear fruit, you are still fruit yourself. Does it say that God severs the fruit? He cuts away the dead parts. Have you ever felt like you had a sin sick area of your life severed so that you could be primed to bear fruit?

John 3:18 says that a person who believes on Jesus is not condemned.

John 6:47 says that if you believe on Jesus you have everlasting life.

Romans 10:13 says whoever shall call on the name of the Lord shall be saved.

1 Corinthians 6:15-21 says we are a temple of the Holy Spirit. (Even if we sin we remain that temple. We simply defile it.)

Ephesians 2:8-10 says that it is a gift free from works that we cannot brag.

None of these are contingent on anything. There are no "ifs" or "might bes."

We are not reconciled by our actions, but by Jesus Christ. Our actions are not considered a factor in our reconciliation. Salvation belongs to our God. We are drawn into eternal life in Him. What is not given independently cannot be lost. Don't you think He'd know we'd lose it if it worked like that?

Philippians 1:6

And I am sure of this, that he who began a good work in you will bring it to completion at the day of Jesus Christ.

Trust Him.

Hebrews 13:5

...for He God Himself has said, I will not in any way fail you nor give you up nor leave you without support. <u>I will not, I will not,</u> I will not in any degree leave you helpless nor forsake nor let you down (relax My hold on you)! Assuredly not!

Believe Him.

Psalm 103:10

He has not dealt with us according to our sins, Nor rewarded us according to our iniquities.

Chick Tip of the Day

Do: Believe that God, who poured out His own blood and allowed Himself murdered to keep covenant with Abraham, can keep covenant with you.

Don't: Believe it is "grace if." It is grace.

DAY 39

Ephesians 5:21-22

"and be subject one to another in the fear of God.

Wives, submit yourselves unto your own husbands, as unto the Lord."

Nobody likes that one. Why is it such a war to submit to our husband, our parent, our boss, or our pastor who just can't seem to get it together by our estimation?

The battle is in the mind, Beloved. It all seems so hard because it is. Our flesh tries to convince us that we are our own god and no one else's way is as good as our way. We are deceived. We have been lied to and made a fool by the world, by our families, by our friends, by our enemies.

May you know that you know, that you know, His Word is true. He is sovereign. He is trustworthy. He would not give you a guideline for turmoil and destruction. He gives a guideline for good. It may not be the safe, easy cookie cutter path that you might desire, but it's the best.

God has designed a way for us to be blessed beyond our imaginations if we would only yield to His will and authority. One of the definitions in the dictionary says submit means to yield to a process. Isn't that a glorious picture? God is changing us often in ways we cannot fathom or understand. We just have to trust that He knows what he is doing. Another definition says to present or propose to another for review, consideration, or decision. Don't you love having a covering? It is your safety net? You can always check yourself with your authority. I love that picture. It reminds me of submitting a paper for school to have my work checked. It is nice to have that pointed out areas we need to work on so that we don't go through life blindly causing harm to others.

What if your authority is ungodly? Submit anyway. May they be turned to the tenderness of Christ by your heart. The definition of submission says to propose an idea. We call that planting seeds. Don't wait in the lurches to attack people with the Word, but in a genuine and loving way share bits of what you are gleaning from what God has told you. Mostly, pray. If your husband is not acting like the beautiful model of Ephesians 5 and evoking your beauty with his word, ask God to make him into that. Never under estimate the power of the Holy Spirit! He only comes in power!

Chick Tip of the Day

Do: Praise Jesus for where you are submitting
Don't: Be discouraged by the enemy for where you have not yet submitted.

DAY 40

I wanted to leave you with a simple word today that will help you in every area of your life. It was taken completely out of context, but I know that it was my word and I am sure it can be applied to you as well. As women we love to talk and we hate to submit. We are not called to gossip, slander, criticize, judge, or tell our husband how to live his life better. We are not called to tell anyone how they can be better at anything. God's Word stands alone and needs no emphasis from you. My advice is that if you cannot say a thing tenderly, do not say it. If pride wells up in you at the thought of correcting or rebuking, do not say the thing. It will eat you alive. God is our avenger. Justice is His.

Not too terribly long ago someone was using scripture to berate my husband in an ungodly way and I was torn up by this person's words. More than anything I wanted to tell them how shallow and hypocritical they were and how blessed and beautiful my husband is. I even wrote out everything I wanted to say. As I was flipping through the Bible, a certain passage stood out to me and a few words in a sentence seemed bigger than the others.

Numbers 12:14

"But the LORD said to Moses, "If her father had but spit in her face, would she not bear her shame for seven days? Let her be shut up for seven days outside the camp, and afterward she may be received again.""

Only five words in that sentence stood out to me and I smiled, thanked God, I let the injustice go. Those five words were, "Let her be shut up." Amen.

Chick Tip of the Day

Do: The thing you were called to do!
Don't: Tarry any longer.

CPSIA information can be obtained at www.ICGtesting.com
Printed in the USA
241483LV00001B/279/A